YARN CRAFTS

By Linda Hetzer

Photographs by Steven Mays

Raintree

Milwaukee ● Toronto ● Melbourne ● London

PROJECT DESIGNS: Weaving, Barbara Jacksier
Stitchery, Madeleine Appell

PRODUCTION: Designer, Deborah Bracken
Illustrators, Lynn Matus and Sally Shimizu
Text editor, Jill Munves

Library of Congress Number: 77-29052

1 2 3 4 5 6 7 8 9 0 82 81 80 79 78

Printed and bound in the United States of America.

Library of Congress Cataloging in Publication Data

Hetzer, Linda.
    Yarn crafts.

    SUMMARY: Easy-to-follow instructions for a
selection of projects involving weaving, string
craft, and stitchery.
    1. Hand weaving — Juvenile literature.
2. Needlework — Juvenile literature.   3. String
craft — Juvenile literature.   4.   Yarn — Juvenile
literature. [1. String craft.   2.   Hand weaving.
3. Needlework.   4. Handicraft] I. Mays, Steven.
II. Shimizu, Sally. III. Matus, Lynn. IV. Title.
TT848.H47   746'.04'7   77-29052
ISBN 0-8172-1176-4

CONTENTS

STRING THINGS

String is such an ordinary item that we rarely think about its many possibilities. If it's thin string, we use it to tie up packages. If it's a thick cord, we use it for hanging out the wash. But string has a lot more than this to offer. By learning some new techniques, you can use string to make unusual designs.

You can stiffen string and make it hold its shape by soaking it in white glue. You can sew it on fabric in much the same way you would embroidery thread. Both techniques are included in the following pages, as are yarn painting and geometric string-art designs.

Yarn painting, the unusual art of decorating an object with string, yarn, or thread, was developed by Central American Indians. Using this technique, you can turn a plain bottle into a colorful vase.

String art is the name we give to geometric designs made with string. The string is wrapped around nails that have been hammered into a plywood board in a geometric shape. The idea behind string art is that curves and circles are made up of a series of straight lines. You secure the string in straight lines from one nail to another, never in a curve. But the end result, as shown opposite, is a circle or a curved line.

String has lots of possibilities. Next time you untie a package, remember to save the string.

MATERIALS

plywood · fabric · yarn · crochet cotton · string · glue · balloons · nails · hammer

String ornaments

You can make a string ornament that looks like a spider's web by gluing string to a balloon. All you need is some white glue, wax paper, petroleum jelly, scissors, a pin, the balloon, and some string.

2 Cut lots of pieces of string for the decoration. The strings can be all different lengths, but make each one at least 12 in. (30.4 cm) long.

1 Blow up a balloon and tie a knot in the end. Next, put a piece of wax paper on your table to protect it. Do all your work on the wax paper.

3 Coat the balloon with a thin layer of petroleum jelly. This will keep the string from sticking to the balloon.

5 When the glue has dried, stick your finger into several of the spaces between the strings. Push the balloon away from the string. Then break the balloon with a pin and pull it out through one of the larger spaces.

4 Pour white glue into a shallow bowl or plate. Dip a piece of string into the glue. Coat the entire piece with glue; then wrap it around the balloon in any design that you want. Continue wrapping glue-covered strings around the balloon until there is more string than balloon showing. Let the balloon dry on the wax paper overnight.

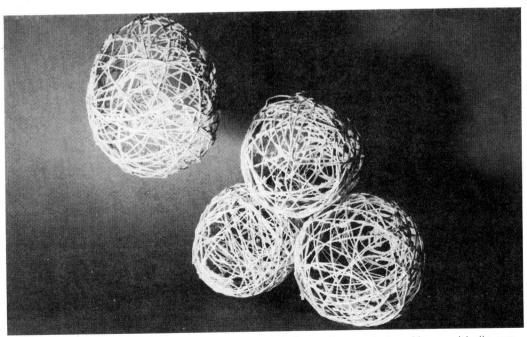

You can tie a string to the ornament and hang it in front of your window. You could pile several string ornaments on a shelf. Or you could hang them on a Christmas tree. Any way you display them, string ornaments are interesting to look at.

String patches

String patches are great for covering holes in jeans, worn-through elbows on jackets, or just for decoration. To make one, you will need colorfast cotton crochet thread, a large-eyed tapestry needle, pencil, ruler, scissors, and an iron-on patch in a color to match the fabric you are going to put it on—all available at variety stores.

2 With a tapestry needle, poke a hole through the fabric at each of the marks. (The fabric is stiff because the back is coated with adhesive. Punching the holes first makes stitching easier.)

1 With a ruler and pencil, draw an angle—two lines that meet—on the patch. If you want a right angle, like the one shown opposite, use the corner of a book as a guide. Make the lines at least 3 in. (7.6 cm) long. Starting at the corner, mark every ¼ in. (.63 cm) along both sides.

3 Thread the needle with a 24-in. (60.9-cm) length of cotton crochet thread. Bring the needle from the back to the front at the last hole on one of the lines. Leave a 2-in. (5-cm) tail on the back of the patch. You do not have to make a knot because the tail will be secure when you iron the patch to the fabric.

6

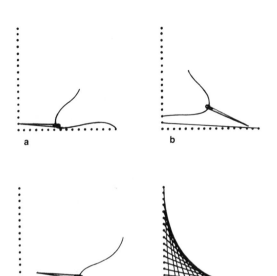

a   b

c   d

4 To start the design, bring the thread to the first hole on the line opposite your starting point (a). Bring the thread through the first hole and up at the second hole in the line. Then bring it back to the next-to-last hole in the first line (b). Go through the fabric at that hole and come up at the next hole. Then bring the thread to the third hole on the other line (c). Continue going from one line to the other this way until all the holes are threaded (d).

6 On the front of the patch, draw another angle. Place it so the ends of the lines meet the ends of the lines from the first angle. Mark every ¼ in. (.63 cm) along both of these lines. Thread this angle the same way you threaded the first angle.

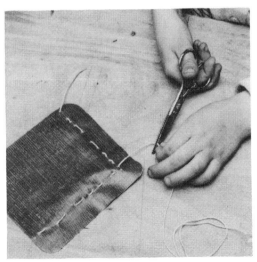

5 When you are done, clip off the excess thread on the back, leaving a 2-in. (5-cm) tail.

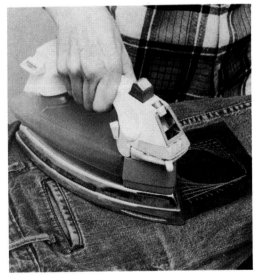

7 Place the patch on your jeans (or other clothing) where you want it to be. Make sure the thread ends are under the patch and iron it to the fabric, following the package directions.

A bright orange string design on a blue denim patch covers a hole in a well-worn pair of blue jeans.

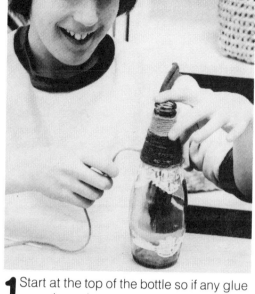

Yarn-painted vases

Yarn painting is a way of creating colorful designs with yarn instead of paint. To create a yarn-painted vase, you will need an empty bottle, white glue, scissors, toothpicks, and yarn scraps in a variety of colors.

Before you decorate the bottle, wash it and peel off as much of the paper label as you can. Let the bottle dry thoroughly before you ap- · ply the glue and yarn.

1 Start at the top of the bottle so if any glue runs down, it won't drip on an area covered with yarn. Put glue all around the top inch of the bottle. To make horizontal stripes, as shown above, glue the end of the yarn to the bottle. Then, holding the yarn taut, turn the bottle so the yarn wraps around it. Be sure you place the rounds of yarn right next to each other so no bottle shows through.

2 To secure the other end of the yarn, put glue on it and place the end against the bottle with a toothpick. (If you use your fingers, the yarn will stick to you rather than the bottle.)

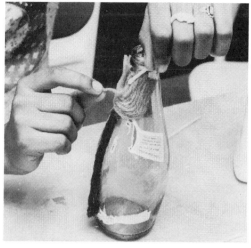

3 To create designs, first outline the shape you want by forming the shape with glue. Then place the yarn over the glue, using a toothpick to help you. Here, a tulip on a stem is being outlined.

4 Then fill in the shape with pieces of yarn that completely cover the bottle. As shown above, the design takes shape from the outside in.

Yarn-painted bottles make great vases for dried flowers. The yarn can be used for gaily colored stripes or for specific designs, like flowers.

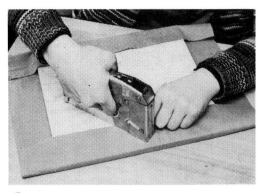

Circular string art

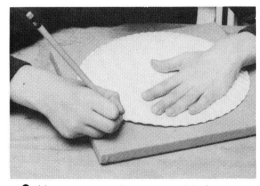

To make a string-art design that has circles within circles, you need a 10 in. (25.4-cm) square of plywood, a 14-in. (35.5-cm) square of cotton fabric, a paper plate, a staple gun, a box of 1-in. (2.5-cm) nails with heads, a hammer, a pencil, white glue, scissors, a hanging loop, and two balls of cotton crochet thread in different colors.

2 Place the board in the middle of the fabric square. Bring the excess fabric on one side around the board and staple it in place. Pull the excess fabric on the opposite side until the fabric on the front is smooth, then staple it to the board. Do this with the other two sides of the board.

3 To get smooth corners, fold the excess fabric at each one into pleats. Put several staples in each corner to hold the pleats firmly in place. Turn the board over so the fabric-covered side faces you.

1 Sand all the edges of the plywood square until they are smooth. Wipe the board with a damp paper towel or rag to remove any sawdust.

4 Use a paper plate as a guide for hammering the nails in a circle. Put the plate in the center of the board. With a pencil, mark every ½ in. (1.2 cm). Or, if the plate has a fluted edge, mark every inden-

tation.

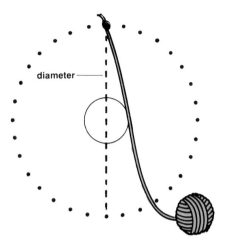

5 Hammer a nail in at each mark in the circle. Hammer the nail halfway into the board, so only ½ in. (1.2 cm) of the nail is visible.

7 To determine where to bring the thread next, hold the board so the nail with the thread is on top. See which nail is directly opposite it. That nail marks the diameter of the circle. If you want to create a small circle in the center of the board, bring the thread to a nail that is three to eight nails to the right of the diameter nail. As shown above, the center of this thread shows you how large the inner circle will be. If you want a larger circle, just move the thread several nails further from the diameter nail.

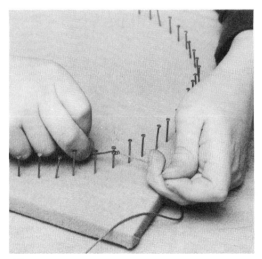

6 Choose the color thread you want to use first and tie it to any nail.

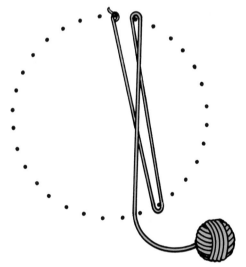

8 Wrap the thread around the nail you choose. Then bring it to the first nail to the *right* of the starting nail, and wrap the thread around that nail. Bring it to the first nail to the *left* of the bottom nail and wrap it around that nail.

11

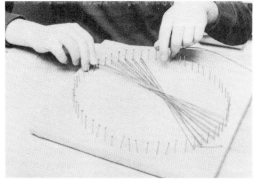

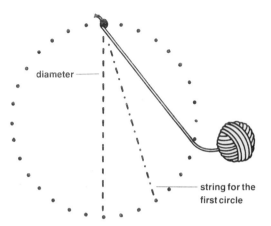

diameter

string for the first circle

9 Continue threading this way, always going from the first unthreaded nail to the right of the starting nail to the first unthreaded nail to the left of the bottom nail. Move the board as needed to work comfortably. Be careful not to catch the thread on any nails except the one you are working with.

12 Take the second color thread and tie the end to the starting nail. To determine the bottom nail, bring the thread to a nail that is somewhere between the starting nail and the nail that was the bottom nail for the first circle. The center of the thread shows you where the edge of the second circle will fall. Wrap the thread around the bottom nail you choose.

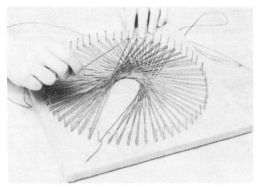

10 When you reach the starting nail, wrap the thread around it again. For the design to work, each nail in the circle must be threaded twice.

11 When you reach the starting nail for the second time, the small circle in the center will be complete. Tie the thread to the starting nail and cut off the excess.

13 Bring the thread from the bottom nail to the first nail to the right of the starting nail. Then bring it to the first nail to the left of the bottom nail. Continue threading this way until you reach the beginning nail for the second time. Tie the end of the thread to the starting nail and cut off the excess.

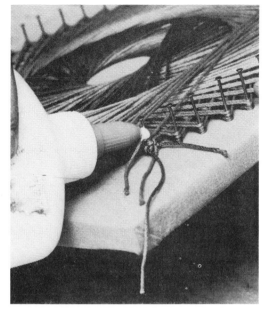

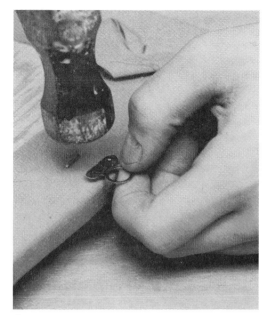

14 Put a few drops of glue on the knots, and let the glue dry overnight. (It will dry clear). Then cut the thread ends very close to the glued knots.

15 If you want to hang the decoration on a wall, turn the board over and hammer a hanging loop into the middle of the top edge.

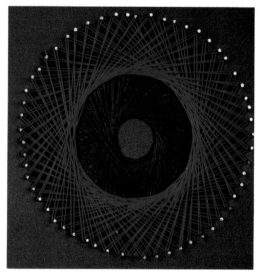

When you thread a round string-art design, you create circles within circles. The size of the inner circles is determined by which nails you choose for threading the first straight line of each circle.

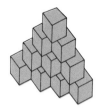

Hexagonal string art

The more intricate a geometric shape you begin with, the more intricate a string-art design you can create with it. A hexagon provides a great many angles that, when threaded, create curves.

To make a hexagonal string-art design, you will need a 12-in. (30.4-cm) square of plywood, a 16-in. (40.6-cm) square of fabric, paper, compass, ruler, and the general string-art materials listed in the circular string-art project.

To start, sand the plywood and cover it with the fabric, following the directions given in the previous project.

2 Place the hexagon pattern on the fabric-covered plywood and center it. Lightly trace around the shape with a pencil. Mark the center of the board by making a pencil mark through the hole the compass made in the center of the paper pattern.

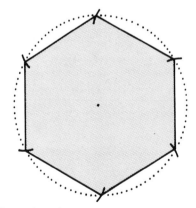

1 To make a hexagon pattern, draw an 11-in. (27.9-cm) circle on the paper. Set your compass to 5½ in. (13.9 cm). Without changing the compass setting, place its point anywhere on the circumference of the circle and make a mark. Put the point on the mark and make another mark. Continue until yu have six marks. Join the marks to get a hexagon. Cut out the shape.

3 With a ruler, mark every ¼ in. (.63 cm) along all six sides of the hexagon.

14

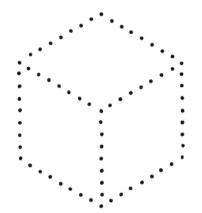

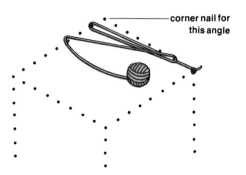

corner nail for
this angle

4 Draw a line from the center point to every corner of the hexagon, as shown above. Mark every ¼ in. (.63 cm) along these three lines

5 Hammer a nail in each of the marks on the nine lines you have drawn. Leave about half of the nail showing.

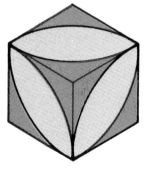

6 Use the first layer of thread for creating shallow curves at each of the six broad angles—three at the edges of the hexagon and three at its center.

7 To begin threading, choose the color thread you want and tie it to the first nail on one line of the angle you are working on. (Work one angle at a time and ignore all the nails not in that angle. Otherwise, the board looks confusing.) For this type of angle, you skip a nail for every nail you wrap. Take the thread from the first nail in the first line to the first nail on the other line. Wrap it around the nail and bring it to the third nail on the first line (leave one nail free). Wrap the thread around the nail and bring it to the third nail on the second line. When you finish threading the angle, do not cut the thread. The end of one angle will be the beginning of the next, so just start the next angle. As shown below, the angles all touch each other because they all share a nail at an outside corner of the hexagon. Work the three outside angles first, then the three inside ones.

8 Continue making these broad curves until you have threaded all six angles. Tie the end of the thread to the beginning nail and cut off the excess.

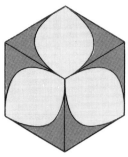

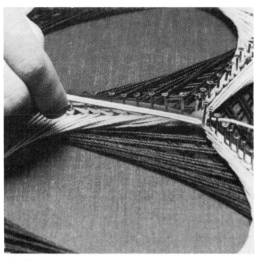

9 With the second layer of thread (use your other color), create a deep curve in each of the six angles along the perimeter of the hexagon. Each pair of angles lies back to back, as shown.

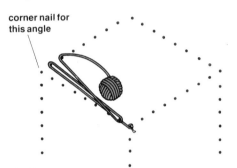

corner nail for
this angle

10 Tie the thread to the center nail. Working with one line on the edge of the hexagon, bring the thread to the first nail on the line, ignoring the corner nail. Bring the thread back to the second nail on the center line. Continue this way until you have threaded all the nails in the angle. Then begin to thread the next angle, following the same steps.

12 Put glue on the beginning and ending knots of both threads. Let the glue dry; then clip off the excess thread. To hang the string art, hammer a hanging loop into the back of the board in the middle of the top edge.

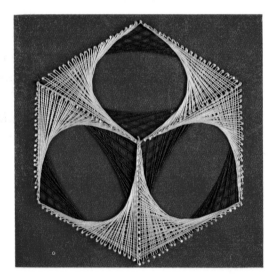

Two sets of angles worked in contrasting thread create a string-art design that looks like a flower. The six broad angles worked in dark brown thread result in shallow curves. The six narrow angles worked in blue thread result in deep curves.

11 The second group of curves will partially cover the first angles. The nails in the center lines are threaded twice because they are each part of two angles. When you finish all six curves, tie the thread to the starting nail.

16

WEAVING

Over and under, over and under. That's all weaving really is, whether you are weaving cloth on a loom that is the size of a room, making a pendant on notched cardboard, or forming a basket. In each of these cases, individual threads are put together in such a way as to form a whole fabric. That is why we weave. There are several terms that are always used to describe the weaving process.

To weave, you interlace a crosswise set of threads called the weft with a lengthwise set of threads called the warp. To make the over-and-under process easier, the warp or lengthwise threads are held taut by a device called a loom. A loom can be a large mechanical one that fills the room. Or it can be a small piece of cardboard with notches cut in it, like the one pictured opposite.

Each project on the following pages is made on a different loom. With a little help, you can make all five of them. The first is a loom made of drinking straws, string, and a dowel. The second loom consists of two crossed sticks; the third of popsicle sticks. Finally, there's a small cardboard loom and one made of canvas stretchers.

How to make the looms and what you can weave with them is shown on the following pages.

MATERIALS

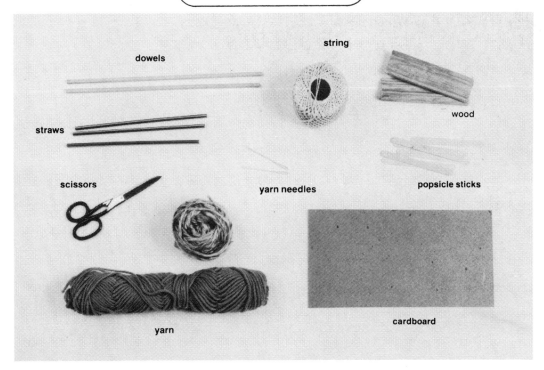

dowels

string

wood

straws

scissors

yarn needles

popsicle sticks

yarn

cardboard

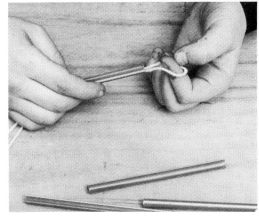

1 Fold each piece of string in half and put the fold through a straw. Gather the four loops together and tie them with a piece of string.

Striped belt

You can make a loom from such things as drinking straws, string, and a dowel. The procedure for setting up this loom is shown in the following photographs.

To make the belt and loom, you need two plastic straws, cut in half; four pieces of string, each twice your waist measurement plus 6 in. (15.2 cm); about 2 oz. (56 g) of rug yarn; scissors; a blunt large-eyed needle; and one or two 12-in. (30.4-cm) dowels, depending on how you set up the loom; and two clothes-pins. The straws are part of the loom. By weaving over them rather than over the strings, you make a belt that is loose and fluffy rather than tight and hard.

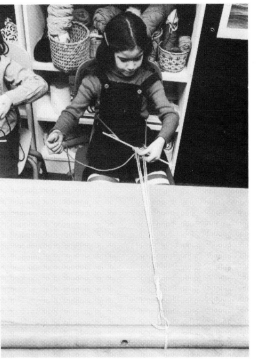

2 To set up the loom, take the string you tied around the loop ends. Tie it to a chair or a dowel that is taped to a table, as shown above. Tie the free ends of the strings to the 12-in. (30.4-cm) dowel. Tie a piece of yarn around one end of the dowel, bring it around your waist, and tie it to the other end of the dowel. Sit away from the loops to keep the strings under tension. Bring the straws near the dowel just in front of you, and you are ready to weave.

3 Cut a 36-in. (91.4-cm) piece of rug yarn and knot the end to two outermost strings at left end of the dowel.

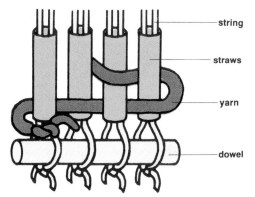

string
straws
yarn
dowel

4 To weave, bring the yarn under the first straw, over the next, under the third, and over the last one. For the next row, starting at the right, bring the yarn under the first straw, over the next, under the next, and over the last one. Continue this way, always going over the straws you went under in the last row, and under those you went over.

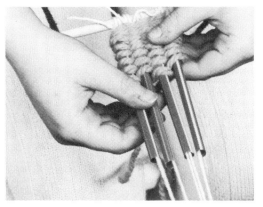

5 The straws are part of the loom; you weave over and under them, not the strings. When the weaving has covered most of the straws, move them up. To do this, hold onto the weaving with your hand. Gently pull the straws with your other hand, leaving just the ends covered by the weaving you have already done. Then continue weaving.

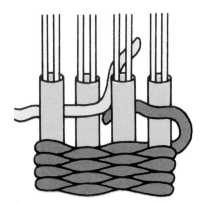

6 If you want to change yarn colors, make the change in the middle of a row, not at the end. When you bring the first color *under* a straw, leave the end behind it. Bring the new color up from the back at the same place, and go over the next straw. Continue weaving with the new color. You can trim the yarn ends when you finish weaving. Follow the same procedure when the first piece of yarn is used up, and you need to add on more.

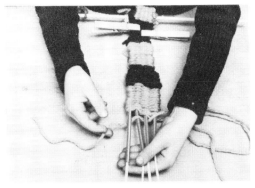

7 As the belt gets longer, it will be difficult to reach the part you're working on. At that point, loosely roll the woven part around the dowel. Hold the top of the weaving to the rolled part with two clothespins.

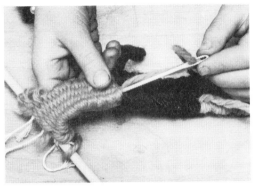

8 When you have woven the length of the strings, untie the dowel from around your waist. Using a large-eyed needle, thread the yarn ends on the back of the belt through the weaving.

9 Untie the looped string ends and slip the straws off them. At the other end, untie the strings from the dowel. Cut the loops in half at the very end, so you have eight strings of equal length at both ends.

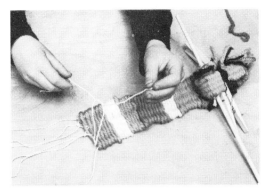

10 The strings become fringe, but first they must be knotted. Leave the first string untied. Then tie the next two strings together. Do the same with the next two strings, and the next two, leaving the last string untied. Do this with the strings at the other end also.

The thick rug yarn used in weaving these belts completely covers the thin string used for warp. The strings show at the ends, however. When the belt is worn, the strings are tied together.

God's-eye

A God's-eye is an ornament used by many Central American Indian tribes to protect them from sickness and evil. You can make one as a decoration for your room. You need two ¼-in. (.63-cm)-thick dowels, each about 9 in. (22.8 cm) long; white glue; and pieces of leftover yarn in a variety of colors.

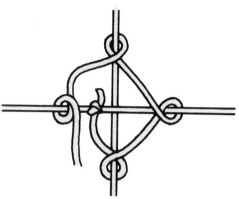

3 To weave the yarn around the sticks, bring the yarn over the first dowel and around it. Bring the yarn to the next dowel, going over and then around it. Continue wrapping the yarn around the dowels this way, as shown above.

1 Lay one dowel on top of the other so they cross in the middle. Put glue in the center to secure them. Wait about half an hour for the glue to dry.

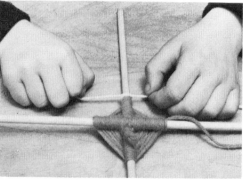

4 To change colors, tie off the first color on one dowel. Tie the new color to the next dowel, and wrap it around the dowels, following the same pattern as before.

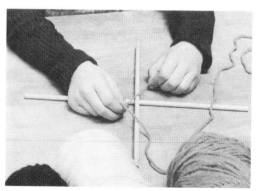

2 Tie one end of a piece of yarn to one of the dowels at the center.

5 When you have finished weaving the yarn around the dowels (leave about 1 in. (2.5 cm) free at the ends), trim the yarn ends and glue them to the dowels on the back of the God's-eye.

A brightly colored God's-eye is an attractive decoration in any room. You could make several in different colors and give them to your friends.

Winter scarf

A back-strap loom is any loom that is strapped or tied around the weaver's back. The weaver's body provides the tension that keeps the wrap threads tight. To make the loom shown here, you need four pieces of wood, each ½ to 1 in. (1.2 to 2.5 cm) thick and 8 in. (20.3 cm) long; nine popsicle sticks; white glue; a hand drill; a 12-in. (30.4-cm) long dowel; a 2-x-8-in. (5-x-20.3-cm) piece of cardboard. For weaving, you need about three 4-oz. (112-g) balls of bulky yarn (two of them for the weft, one for the warp); and two clothespins.

1 For the loom, ask an adult to drill a hole in the center of each popsicle stick. Put glue along one flat side of two pieces of wood. Put the popsicle sticks on the glued wood, as shown, keeping the holes in an even line.

2 Put glue on the other two pieces of wood and place them on top of the first two pieces. Let the glue dry overnight.

3 To make a shuttle, a tool for holding the weft yarn, cut a triangular notch in each end of the piece of cardboard. Wrap yarn around the length of the cardboard, fitting it in the notches. When the shuttle will hold no more yarn, clip the end from the ball of yarn.

5 To secure the warp threads to the loom, tie the yarn ends at front end of the loom to the 12-in. (30.4-cm) dowel. On the other end, gather the threads together and tie them to the back of a chair or a second dowel taped to the table.

4 To set up the loom, cut 17 pieces of yarn, each twice as long as you want your scarf. These are the warp. Thread one through each space between the popsicle sticks and one through each hole.

6 To complete the loom, tie the 12-in. (30.4-cm) dowel around your waist and sit far enough away from the table to pull the warp threads taut. To start weaving, put the weft through the warp threads leaving a 2-in. (5-cm) tail at the side.

7 This loom makes weaving over and under the threads easy because it separates them. To weave over the threads that go through the holes in the popsicle sticks, push down on the loom. This will lower the threads that go through the sticks and raise the ones that go between them. Hold the raised threads with your hand, and put the shuttle carrying the weft thread through the space between the groups of threads. (This loom was threaded in two different colors so you can see the two groups of threads. You can use one color warp if you want.)

9 After you have woven back and forth several times, pull the loom toward you. The loom will press the threads together so the weaving is compact. Change yarn colors whenever you like, leaving a 2-in. (5-cm) tail at the side when you do. When you finish weaving, you can thread these ends through the scarf with a large-eyed needle.

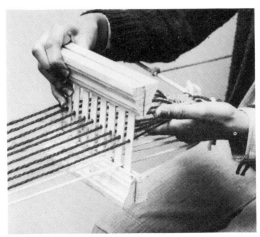

8 To weave under the threads that go through the popsicle sticks, pull up on the loom. These threads will now be above the threads that go through the spaces between popsicle sticks. Pass the weft or filling thread through the space. Continue weaving by first pushing down on the loom and passing the yarn through the space, then pulling up on the loom and putting the yarn through.

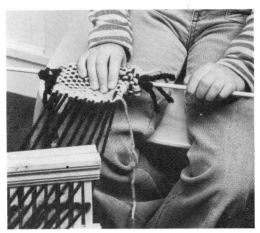

10 As the weaving progresses, making it difficult for you to reach the loom, roll the woven scarf around the dowel and hold it in place with a clothespin on each side.

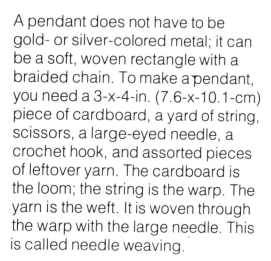

11 When you have finished weaving, untie the warp threads at both ends of the loom. Knot the warp threads so the weaving does not ravel. Trim these ends for fringe.

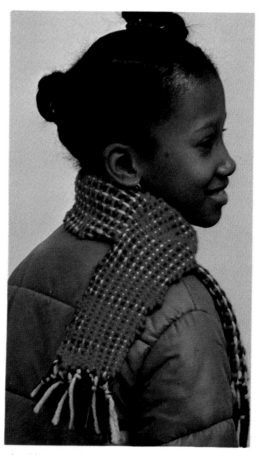

Jackie proudly models the scarf that she wove on a back-strap loom. She chose colors in the same family—brown and yellow for the warp and orange for the weft—to create a tweed scarf.

Woven pendant

A pendant does not have to be gold- or silver-colored metal; it can be a soft, woven rectangle with a braided chain. To make a pendant, you need a 3-x-4-in. (7.6-x-10.1-cm) piece of cardboard, a yard of string, scissors, a large-eyed needle, a crochet hook, and assorted pieces of leftover yarn. The cardboard is the loom; the string is the warp. The yarn is the weft. It is woven through the warp with the large needle. This is called needle weaving.

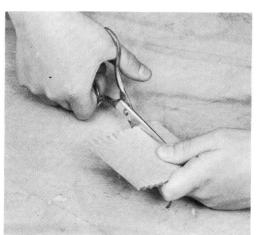

1 Make a mark every ¼ in. (.63 cm) along both short sides of the cardboard. With a pair of scissors, make a notch at each of the marks.

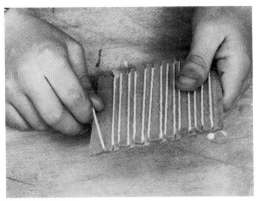

2 Slip one end of the string into the first notch, and tape the end to the back of the cardboard. Bring the string to the notch opposite the first one. Then slip it behind the cardboard and bring it out at the next notch. Bring it back to the opposite notch. Continue putting the string on the cardboard this way. After the last notch, tape the end to the back of the cardboard.

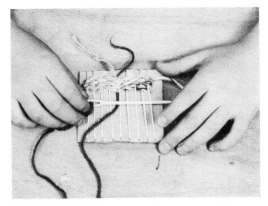

4 When you want to change to a different color yarn, thread the end of the first color down through the weaving in the center. Bring the second color up through the weaving in the same space that you ended the first color. Continue weaving that row with the new color. You can trim these ends later.

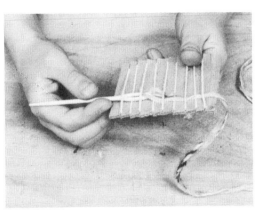

3 To weave, thread a piece of yarn through the large-eyed needle, and bring the needle over and under the string warp. Beat the weft down tightly with your fingers every third or fourth row.

5 When you finish, thread the end of the yarn through the weaving. Take the weaving off the cardboard by slipping the string off the notches. The weaving has finished edges on all sides except for the beginning and end of the string that was taped to the cardboard. Slip these ends through the nearest weft thread, knot them, and trim the ends.

6 The string loops will show at the top and bottom of the rectangle. Push the weaving over them on both sides. If you beat the weft down tightly enough during the weaving, there will be enough yarn to cover them. On the back of the weaving, trim all the yarn ends.

9 To make the braided chain, cut three pieces of yarn that are one and a half times longer than the chain you want. Tie the ends to a doorknob. Bring the right thread over the center, then the left over the center. Continue this way, leaving 2 in. (5 cm) free at the bottom. Slip the ends of the braid through the top right and left corners of the woven rectangle. On the back, knot the braid ends to a weft thread and trim them.

7 To make fringe, cut yarn to twice the length you want the fringe to be. Fold each piece in half. Put a crochet hook through the bottom row of the weaving. Put the fold on the hook and pull it through.

8 Slip the ends of the fringe through the loop and pull them tight. Repeat this procedure along the bottom edge of the weaving.

You can transform small pieces of leftover yarn into a pendant by weaving them on a cardboard loom. Fringe and braided chain complete this soft piece of jewelry.

Woven tapestry

You can make a woven wall hanging, called a tapestry, on a simple frame loom. To make the loom, you will need two sets of canvas stretchers (available at art-supply stores)—one set for the length and one for the width; a box of 1-in. (2.5-cm) nails with heads; one ball of cotton crochet thread; a ruler; a hammer; a fork; a cardboard shuttle (as described in the scarf project); and a staple gun.

You can make the tapestry any size. The amount of yarn needed will vary with the size frame used. We used a 12-x-24-in. (30.4-x-60.9-cm) frame and needed 8 oz. (226 g) of bulky and novelty yarn.

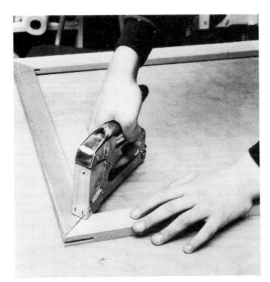

1 To make the frame, slip the corners of the canvas stretchers together. Reinforce the corners by putting two or three staples through each.

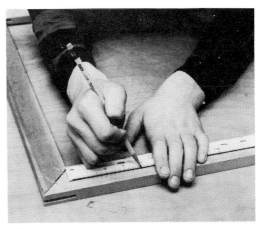

2 Decide on the width tapestry you want. Measure off this width on the top and bottom of the frame, centering it between the sides. Mark every ¼ in. (.63 cm) across the width. (The finished weaving will be slightly smaller than the width you mark on the frame because the weaving pulls in somewhat.)

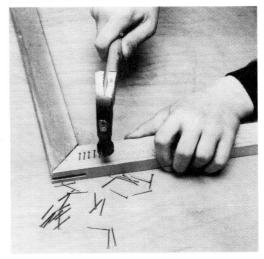

3 Hammer a nail through each of the marks on both the top and bottom of the frame. Hammer them in only halfway, so about ½ in. (1.2 cm) of the nail is still visible.

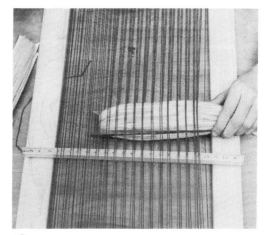

4 To put the warp thread on the loom, tie one end to the first nail. Bring the thread to the opposite nail, then back to the second nail, then to the second nail on the opposite side. Continue threading this way until you have covered all the nails. Tie the thread to the last nail.

6 Turn the ruler on its side to create a space between the warp threads. Put the shuttle with the weft yarn through this space. Leave about 2 in. (5 cm) of yarn at the beginning.

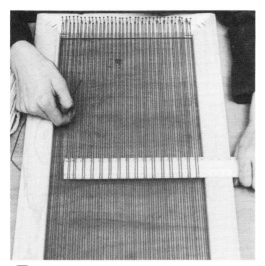

7 Turn the ruler flat and use a fork to beat the weft yarn in place.

5 To prepare for weaving, wrap the yarn you will use around the cardboard shuttle. Weave the ruler over two threads, and under two across the loom. (The warp threads are used in pairs because the yarn used for weft or filling is much thicker than the crochet cotton used for the warp.)

8 With the ruler still flat, weave the shuttle over and under the warp threads again. Go over the threads you went under and under the ones you went over in the previous row.

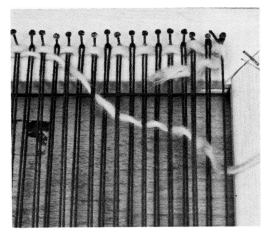

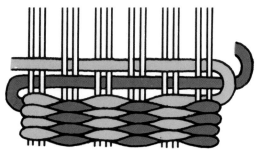

9 To secure the beginning end of the thread, weave it over and under the first few warp threads before you beat in the second row of weft thread. Continue weaving, alternating these two rows. As you change yarn colors, secure the yarn ends as shown above.

11 To make vertical stripes in the weaving, weave one row of the first color, one row of the second color. Alternate these two rows. When you beat in the yarns, they will form vertical stripes.

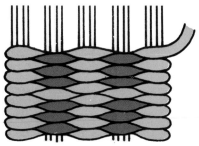

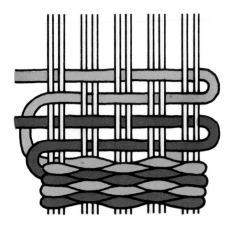

12 To make a geometric design combining both horizontal and vertical stripes, alternate the first and second colors for six rows (three rows of each color). This will create vertical stripes. Weave three rows of the first color to form a horizontal stripe. Then alternate the second and first colors for another six rows to make vertical stripes again.

10 To make thin horizontal stripes in the weaving, weave two rows of one color, then two rows of a second color. Continue alternating these rows for as many stripes as you want. To make thick horizontal stripes, weave four or more rows of one color, then four or more rows of the second color. If you are not using one color of weft yarn for several rows, leave it on the side and simply pick it up again when you want to use it. If you are not going to use it for several inches (cm), cut it off and weave the end in as shown above.

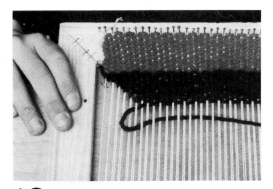

13 To create a diagonal design, weave one color of yarn, bringing the yarn over one less set of warp threads with each row. You can continue doing this until you go over only one set of warp threads. The weaving will create a diagonal line across the warp threads.

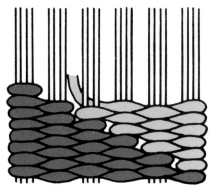

14 To fill in the diagonal area with a second color, begin weaving on the opposite side of the loom. Weave over one set of warp threads on the first row, two sets in the second row. Continue this way until the second color fills the diagonal and can be woven across an entire row.

15 Before you remove the tapestry from the loom, weave a weft thread over one warp and under one so the weaving does not ravel. Then lift the strings off the nails and push the weaving up to cover the string. You can press it lightly with a steam iron.

Both these tapestries were woven on the same kind of loom, but Gabrielle used a subtle color scheme worked in small, intricate patterns (left) to produce a tapestry very different from Bryan's, in which bright, bold colors were woven in a large geometric design (right).

STITCHERY

Stitchery, another name for embroidery, is a method of decorating fabric with needle and thread. It is a broad name that includes many stitches and a variety of materials.

Cross-stitch and appliqué are two types of stitchery you will find on the following pages. You will also find a sampler you can make. In cross-stitch, you use thread to make decorative X s on fabric; in appliqué, you use a running stitch to sew cut-out fabric pieces onto a larger piece of cloth. In making a sampler, you use many different stitches to form a design on fabric.

The fabric you use in stitchery depends on what you are making. For cross-stitch, use gingham, a checkered lightweight cotton. When you do appliqué work, use felt. For a sampler, the stripes in pillow ticking will help determine the design.

For stitching, use embroidery thread or knitting yarn. With embroidery thread, you will need to use embroidery needles, which are sharp-pointed, small-eyed needles that slide through fabric easily. With knitting yarn, use large-eyed needles so you can thread the yarn through the eye easily. You will also need small sharp scissors to cut the thread and an embroidery hoop to keep the fabric stretched tight. An embroidery hoop consists of two wooden or metal rings. To use one, lay the fabric on the smaller circle. Place the larger circle on top of the fabric and press down.

MATERIALS

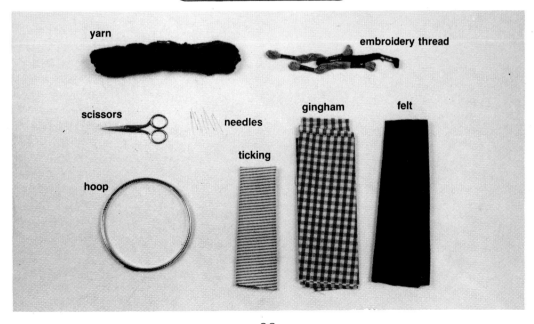

yarn

embroidery thread

scissors

needles

gingham

felt

ticking

hoop

Cross-stitch belt

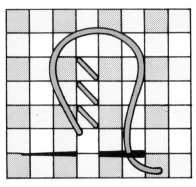

Cross-stitch is easy to do on gingham fabric because the squares in the fabric guide you when you make the stitches. To make a cross-stitch, you make an X that fills a square from corner to corner.

To make the belt shown on the following page, you will need a piece of felt 3 in. (7.6 cm) wide and long enough to go around your waist, a piece of ginham that is 3 in. (7.6 cm) wide and about 4 in. (10.1 cm) shorter than the felt, embroidery thread, needles, and yarn. As a guide for making your name or initials, you will need graph paper and pencil.

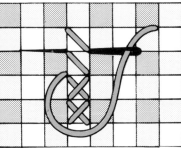

2 To make a row of cross-stitches, start at the top X. Bring the needle from the back of the material out to the front at the top left corner of the X. Go in at the bottom right corner and come out again at the top left corner of the next X. You have made the first half of a cross-stitch. Continue working the same way until you reach the bottom of the row (top). Then, starting at the bottom stitch, fill in the second half of the Xs. Bring the needle from the bottom left corner to the top right corner, coming up again at the bottom left corner for the next stitch (bottom). Complete the second half of the cross-stitches in this row before going on to the next row.

1 On graph paper, draw the letters in your name or initials. Then fill the letters with X s as Kristina is doing. Each square on the paper gets one X.

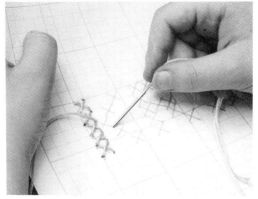

3 Practice the cross-stitch, working right on the graph paper.

4 With a pencil, lightly draw the Xs for your name or initials on the gingham.

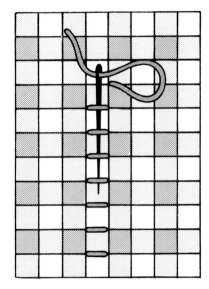

6 When you finish stitching or run out of thread, bring the needle and thread under the last several stitches on the back. Cut the thread close to the stitches. Do the same thing with the extra thread you left at the beginning. This secures the thread without a knot.

5 Start stitching on the gingham. Don't knot the thread, but leave several extra in. (cm) on the back.

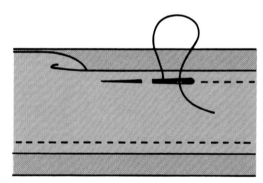

7 Make a ½-in. (1.2-cm) hem along all four edges of the gingham, ironing it to keep the fabric in place. Then center the gingham on the felt. With a needle and embroidery thread, make a running stitch around the edges of the gingham, securing it to the felt. As shown above, a running stitch is simply a line of stitches that run along the edges of the fabric.

8 When you finish the running stitch around all four sides of the gingham, end the thread by knotting it on the back.

10 Fold an 18-in. (45.7-cm) piece of yarn in half and put the fold through the hole from the back. Loop the ends of the yarn through the fold and pull them tight. Do this with the other three holes.

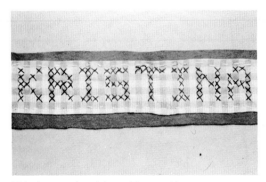

Kristina embroidered her entire name on the belt, using four different colors of embroidery thread.

9 With a hole punch, make two holes at both ends of the felt. Make each hole ½-in. (1.2-cm) from the end.

The yarn pieces are tied in a bow to secure the belt. Hillary tied her belt in the back so her initials, H.K., are visible on the front.

Appliquéd poncho

You can make an attractive poncho from felt of one color and decorate it with felt designs in a contrasting color. The decorative pieces are sewn to the poncho with a running stitch. They do not need to be hemmed because felt does not fray.

To make a poncho that fits, tape newspaper together to make a 28-in. (71.1-cm) square. Using the steps that follow, cut out the neck opening. Try on the paper pattern. If it is too big, make your original square a few inches (cm) smaller. If the poncho is too small, make a larger square out of newspaper.

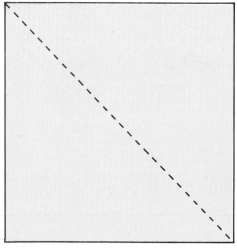

1 Cut a 28-in. (71.1-cm) square (or the right size for you) out of felt. Fold it in half diagonally as shown by the dotted line.

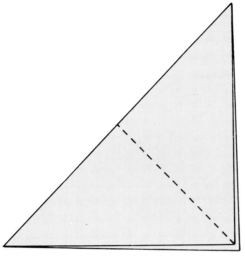

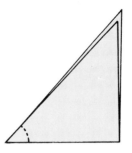

4 To make the neck opening, draw a curved line that is 3 in. (7.6 cm) from the corner that is the center of the original square. Cut along the line you have drawn.

2 Fold the new triangle in half on the dotted line.

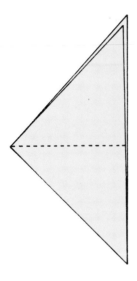

3 Fold this new triangle in half, again following the dotted line.

5 To make a pattern for the cut-out decorations, fold a piece of paper into quarters and cut a fancy edge. You can cut a piece out of the center also, as Dana did, to make a snowflake shape.

 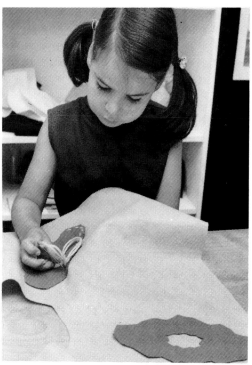

6 Using a felt-tipped marker, trace the pattern on the second color felt, then cut out the shape.

7 Pin the shape to your poncho. With yarn and a large-eyed needle, sew it to the poncho with a running stitch.

Dana, Susannah, and Kristina are three proud designers as they model the appliquéd felt ponchos they made.

40

Desk set

You can make a desk set—a matching pad and pencil holder—out of ordinary things you have around the house, such as cardboard, a pad, white glue, and an empty juice can. To decorate the set, you will need about ½ yd. (45.7 cm) of felt, yarn in several colors, and some large-eyed needles.

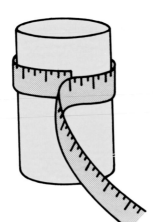

2 With a ruler and pencil, mark off these pieces on the felt, then cut out each piece, as Jason is doing.

1 You will need three pieces of felt in all. To determine the size of the first piece, measure the height of the can and its width, going around the can with a tapemeasure. Add 2 in. (5 cm) to both measurements. For the other two pieces, measure the pad. For the top piece, you will need felt 1 in. (2.5 cm) longer and wider than the pad. For the bottom piece, you will need felt that is 6 in. (15.2 cm) longer and wider than the pad.

3 On the felt for the can, mark off the extra inch (2.5 cm) on top and bottom. Using yarns of different colors, decorate the felt between the lines with a running stitch.

4 Put white glue around the entire can.

5 Place the can on the back of the felt, centering the can from top to bottom. Roll the can so the felt sticks to the glue, being careful not to get glue on the front of the felt.

6 Clip the extra felt on the top and bottom of the can, allowing about 1 in. (2.5 cm) between cuts. You will end up with a series of felt flaps.

7 On the top edge of the can, put glue on each of these flaps and push the flaps to the inside of the can. Hold them for a few minutes until the glue dries.

8 On the bottom of the can, put glue on each flap and hold it against the bottom until the glue dries. Overlap the flaps so they all fit.

9 To make the pad cover, glue the small piece on top of the big piece of felt. This will form a pocket you can slip the pad into. To start, put glue around three sides of the smaller piece of felt, leaving one short edge free of glue.

12 Cut a piece of cardboard 2 in. (5 cm) longer and wider than your pad. Turn the pad cover and center the cardboard on it. Put glue around all the edges of the cardboard.

10 Center the small piece on the large one. The glue will hold it in place temporarily as you stitch.

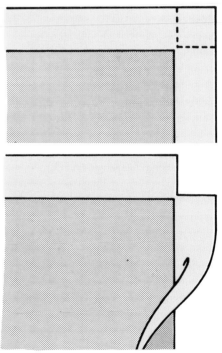

11 With yarn and a large-eyed needle, make a running-stitch decoration around the three glued sides of the pocket, going through both layers of felt. The stitches are decorative and also hold the two pieces of the pad cover together.

13 To make a neat edge, cut out the corners of the felt along the dotted lines (top). Don't cut right up to the cardboard. Leave a ¼-in. (.63-cm) space. Fold the felt over the cardboard (bottom). Hold it a few minutes until the glue dries. Then turn the felt over and slip the cardboard backing of the pad into the pocket.

This matching pad and pencil holder are handsome as well as useful additions to anyone's desk.

Sampler

In earlier times, children learned the art of embroidery by making a sampler of lots of different stitches. You can make a modern version of a sampler and turn it into a pillow or a wall hanging. To make a 12-in. (30.4-cm) pillow or hanging, you will need a 13-in. (33-cm) square of pillow ticking, embroidery thread in lots of colors, needles, scissors, and an embroidery hoop. For a pillow, you will need a 13-in. (33-cm) square of felt for the backing and polyester stuffing. For a wall-hanging, you will need 12-in. (30.4-cm) canvas stretchers (available at art stores) and a staple gun. Shown at right and on the following page are stitches you can use in your sampler.

For the **straight stitch**, bring the needle up from the back of the fabric where you want the stitch to begin. Put the needle back in where you want the stitch to end, bringing it out at the beginning of the next stitch.

The **stem or outline stitch** is a series of slanted stitches lying next to each other. To start the stitch, bring the needle out from the back of the fabric where you want the bottom of the stitch to be. Put it in again at the top, making a slanted stitch. Come out again at the bottom of the next stitch.

For the **chain stitch**, bring the needle to the front of the fabric at the top of the stitch. Put the needle back in the fabric just to the right of where it came out and bring it out at the top of the next stitch. Loop the thread around the needle, as shown, before you pull it through the fabric.

44

For the **split stitch**, bring the needle out to the front of the fabric. Put the needle back in to the right of where it came out. Bring the needle out just to the left of where it went in, and go through the thread, splitting it as shown.

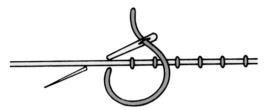

The **couching stitch** requires two pieces of thread. Lay one piece down on the fabric. With the second—or working— thread, make small stitches, ¼ in. (.63 cm) apart, from the bottom to the top of the first thread to secure it to the fabric.

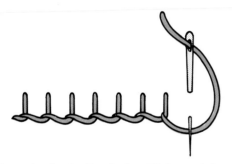

To make the **buttonhole stitch**, work from left to right. Bring the needle up at the left side of the stitch. Put the needle in at the top right and bring it out at the bottom right, catching the thread under the needle. The stitches can be close together or far apart; they can be the same height or different heights.

To make a **French knot**, bring the needle out to the front of the fabric where you want the stitch to be. Wrap the thread around the needle three or four times, then put the needle back in the fabric, close to where you brought it out.

The **herringbone stitch** consists of a series of slanted stitches that cross each other. To make the stroke that slants upward, bring the needle up at the bottom left of the stitch. Put the needle in at the top right. Bring it out slightly to the left of where you put it in to start the next stroke, as shown. Then put the needle in at the bottom right to complete the stroke that slants downward and bring it out to the left to start the next stitch that slants upward.

To make a **sheaf stitch**, make three straight stitches that are parallel to each other. Bring the needle up in the center behind the stitches and slide the needle out between the stitches and the fabric. Bring the thread around the stitches and put the needle back in at the center. Pull this last stitch tight to wrap the stitches like a sheaf of wheat.

The **fly stitch** consists of large horizontal stitches secured in the center by small vertical stitches. Bring the needle up at the left side of the stitch. Insert the needle at the right of the stitch, then bring it out at the center, as shown. Catch the thread under the needle. To complete the stitch, put the needle back into the fabric to make a vertical stitch. Then bring it out on the left side to begin the next stitch.

3 Turn the pillow cover right side out and fill it with stuffing.

1 To start your sampler, put an embroidery hoop on your fabric. Use embroidery thread in different colors to work different stitches in the white stripes, using any of the stitches shown on the last two pages.

4 Fold under the edges of the opening, pin it closed, and stitch it.

2 When you have finished the embroidery, decide if you want to make a pillow or a wall hanging. To make a pillow, place the embroidery face down on the backing fabric. Stitch around all four sides, leaving a 5-in. (12.7-cm) opening on one side. Trim the corners.

5 To make a wall hanging, place the embroidery face down and put the canvas stretcher on top. Staple one side of the fabric to the wooden stretcher. To make it taut, staple the opposite side. Then staple the two remaining sides.

Whether you make your embroidered sampler into a pillow or a wall hanging, you will have a lasting record of your stitches that you can refer to for future projects.

Your own monogram

One personal way to use your stitchery skills is to embroider your initials on a favorite piece of clothing. To make an interesting monogram (a design made up of your initials), draw your initials on paper. Combine them in different ways until you are pleased with the design.

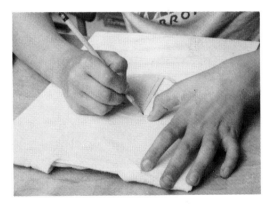

1 Fold the garment over a piece of cardboard for a firm backing as you draw the monogram on the fabric with a pencil.

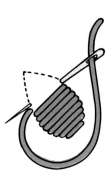

2 If you want to completely cover an area of the design, use the **satin stitch**. First draw the shape you want with a pencil. Then bring the needle out at the bottom of the stitch. Put it in at the top, bringing it out again at the bottom of the next stitch. Each stitch fills the area so the size of the stitches will vary according to the width of the outline. The stitches should lie next to each other with no fabric showing between them.

3 Put an embroidery hoop on the area you want to embroider, and stitch the design.

Gabrielle embroidered block letters on the back yoke of her jacket and added a raccoon and a flower to complete the design. Lauren worked her initials on the front pockets of her jacket, while Bryan made a large monogram in the center of his T-shirt.

48